Not Saying Goodbye
at Gate 21

Not Saying Goodbye
at Gate 21

Kathleen Jones

Templar Poetry

Published in 2011 by Templar Poetry

Templar Poetry in an imprint of Delamide & Bell

Fenelon House

Kingsbridge Terrace

58 Dale Road, Matlock, Derbyshire

DE4 3NB

www.templarpoetry.co.uk

ISBN 978-1-906285-14-2

A CIP catalogue record of this book is available from the British Library

Typeset by Pliny
Graphics by Paloma Violet

Printed in India

For Neil

Acknowledgements

The Soul Catcher, Outposts; *The View from Here, The Silence of Snow*, Pitch; *Whale Music*, Other Poetry; *The Fell Gate*, Chapman; *Ginny,* The North; *An Emphasis of Want,* MsLexia; *Aiming for Archangel, Tycho de Brahe, Above Middleton,* The Tabla Book of New Verse; *Adopted, To the Gods the Shades,* Lancaster Litfest Anthology; *War Hero*, Sheffield Thursday; *Enemy Territory,* Tears in the Fence; *Terremoto, The Reluctant Moon* on the on-line site 'The Tuesday Poem'. *Ginny* was used in the film 'The Mind of Man'. Seven poems were part of a sequence exhibited for Visual Arts Year 1999 with photographer Tony Riley. Four other poems, *Queen Meave, Elizabeth's Story, Glasnost, On Leaving Children*, were also previously published in 'Unwritten Lives'.

Contents

Aiming for Archangel: Lake Onega

We're far north;
beyond the setting point of the sun
which rims the horizon
as though it could always be summer.

Late July, and the birch trees
shift and shiver at three am
in a wind straight from Murmansk
and the perpetual arctic ice.

From the lake's edge the land seems
to go on forever - beyond politics,
into the impossible distances
of history, where women still

wash their clothes in the stream
and sleep above the stove.
Their children crowd the landing stage
with jars of wild strawberries,

flash stainless-steel teeth
at my bad Russian, show me
their living space above the cows—
a garden fenced with chopped logs,

cellars of potatoes stacked
against the fixed line where the sun sets
and the long winter night closes
over the trees like an eye-lid.

Facing Elsinore

Tycho de Brahe (Astronomer) 1546-1601

Once he lived in Hamlet country,
Sorcerer's Island between
Helsingborg and Elsinore.
And though the King has pulled down
his observatory,
Tycho observed everything.

I have written it down
as he told me.

Since then we have travelled like a circus;
myself the clown
and he, not the least
of the animals,
following the new star
that burned for two days and nights
over Denmark,

fixed
in his calculations —

unlike the Elk
who drank his beer
fell down the tower stairs
and died,
whose extravagant antlers
he remembered - every curve.
Or the bodies of women
and the poems he inked
on his own press
whose variable measures
he abandoned

for the exact constellations
of stars.

2

Such certainty is blasphemous.
But I have watched how he
translates the whirling heavens
to spheres of wood and brass,
rotates them at the turn of a crank,
notching their numbers on the oak
beams of his quadrant,
resting the optic glass
against his silver nose—
fashioned to bridge
the distance of a bullet
that ended friendship—

something he could not calculate.

While he framed horoscopes for Queens,
flattered the Landgrave's wife
with astral fictions
and quarrelled with Kepler,
his friend the Bear was stealing
his model of the universe.
Leaving him only
a new star, half a comet
and the mathematics of age.

His last eclipse less predictable than the first.

Tycho de Brahe,
who told a king's son once
to piss off - forfeiting his pleasure
and thirty thousand shillings—
is dying of politeness.
He stayed too long at court
neglecting to relieve himself
until his body had forgotten how.

3

His brain, drowning in alcohol and piss,
facing a certainty beyond the measure
of his astrolabe,
remembers only Latin now:
ne frusta vixisse videar
"Let not my life be wasted",
pleading as if he knew
his rival, Kepler, waits outside
for an Imperial messenger,
using his instruments and
writing a letter
to Galileo.

I am only the dwarf Jepp,
but I have written it all down
as he told me.

Glasnost

I try to pretend it isn't happening.
Posing in front of Lenin's tomb
for happy snaps, the fake smile
hides a mistake as big as Siberia.

Later, at the Stalin Dock
we sit on deck and drink Champanskoe
watching the sun set in the Volga
with no language to communicate
that isn't compromised. The politics of love
suddenly incorrect between us.

And two more weeks in cramped quarters
watching the pine and birch repeat
mile after mile towards the Arctic Circle's
clear, perpetual daylight.

The Silence of Snow

I live inside the silence of snow —
guarding my steps precariously

Snowlight hollows out the house
enlarging distances —

in the silence and the distance
I hear my life falling,

soft and cold and insistent as snow.
We avoid touch, eye contact —

language flakes against the glass,
monosyllables of ice.

In the dark, an unfamiliar landscape
whitens beyond the window.

I imagine solitary snow fields.
A single line of prints.

Under the duvet's white drifts
we trespass unconsciously —

a sleeping thaw that threatens
waking separation.

Outside, snow crumbles quietly
from an invisible sky.

The Fell Gate

Hung between stone monoliths
framing a postcard view
it marked the limits of our territory.

At six I swung, forbidden
wedging my toe caps in the sheep wire
nailed to the wood, watching
my father and his circling dogs
driving them in across
the nape of the fell
ready to hitch and drag it open
at his whistle.

Taller, I climbed it
racing for the ridge
through fox-coloured tussock grass
and nesting curlews
avoiding the green mires
deep enough to drag a horse down;
warned against abandoned mines,
houses with eyeless lintels
and the ghost of Sworley
wife-murderer,
who hanged himself in the barn.

Now, with the farm empty
the gate dislocated from its hinges
and the fields tussocking over
with rush and gorse, I pass
through its open cromlech
into a tourist's landscape.
Still able to feel

the hitch and drag of it
in my hands,
strong enough to pull
a whole life down.

Ginny

The brothers
swill the farm dirt
from their torsos
at the kitchen sink
and sit at table
watching their sister
lift the heavy silver pot
to pour the tea.

Embroidered hollyhocks and roses frame
the text upon the parlour wall.
`*Christ is the Head of this House*
The Invisible Guest at every meal.'

Ginny carves the bread against her breast
dealing the slices to her brothers
seeing her father's shadow at their backs
putting her school prize on the fire.

The parlour clock ticks away the unused time.
Hollyhocks smother the window's light
to a green dusk.
Ginny smooths her grey reflection
in the teapot's face
passing her brothers the cake
without a word.

Adopted

Her mother told her she was chosen,
lifted from a row of cots containing
inconvenient babies; a charitable home
hopeless with the sound of crying.

The girl who birthed her, knitted
jackets trimmed with thin, white ribbon,
embroidered gowns. Stitched her name
'Anne' into the flannelette. For weeks after,

she'd kept on coming to the house,
begging to see her child. Just once,
to hold her, look at her. Left behind
a letter blotched, unreadable.

Annie knew nothing. Only that she'd been
a waitress in a seaside café. So we spent
weekends and holidays drinking unwanted
milkshakes. Looking for likenesses.

When the law changed she was given
a bad address in London. High-rise blocks
with sour stairs, dog shit on the landings.
Found a thin, tired woman with limp hair

crying, clutching a crumpled photograph.
So unlike her they had to be mistaken.
But then, there was the letter and the name—
all that grief and twenty five years distance,

not to be wished away by birthday or Christmas
cards and the occasional visit. They sit
politely in a tea shop, neither family nor friends,
compelled by the ruthless connection of genes.

Severe Weather

He kept his father's paintings in the attic;
remnants of a life, carefully catalogued.

Lived in two rooms (out of thirty five).
The bedroom, carpeted with copies of The Times;

the library - each precious book dust-free
behind the glass. He spent his days there

editing his father's work, collecting letters,
the scholarly biography - his own

a footnote to the text. A felt hat
in the hall. Unused galoshes. The sunken

garden terraced with ivy, where once he
entertained young boys to tea, read poetry,

and when they married, gave expensive gifts—
letting the roof drip into buckets.

Wore gloves around the house, two waistcoats
and an overcoat. In desperation piled

the bedroom fireplace high to smoulder
the old joists and a lifetime's printed paper

into a conflagration even the rain,
driving through broken slates
found it impossible to douse.

River Rising

From the window
the weir's constant conversation
has vanished—
levelled
by a brown silence.

We watch the water push
its way around the mill house
dangerous and unexpected.
Measure its rise
step over step
towards the door.

We rescue carpets
stack sandbags. Decide
what we most value.

Gently it laps across
the flagstones, casually
exploring cupboards, cellars
boot-deep. Then—
a thud, a surge; the force
that drove the mill wheels powers
through windows and doors.

From the safe stairs' island
we fish floating furniture
with a broom. All our geography
is different - now we are
part of the river's narrative.

It rushes through rooms,
every window's view;
everything is river.

Beyond the gaping doors
a street lamp blooms
yellow in a brown sea.

Heron

I am the River God.

A hunched Egyptian in the
reed-frieze of the river margin.

My legs are armoured against
the jaws of the fabulous Pike.

No frog or salmon fry escapes
the swift Samurai of my beak.

I stand erect in the Book of the Dead.
I am the winged Soul of the Pharaoh

rising up from the water.
My faults are all in my belly.

War Hero

Grandfather was a war-hero
with gas-scarred lungs and muscles
lumpy with shrapnel.

"Feel them," he'd order
stretching his mutilated arm.
I touched reluctantly.

My grandmother curtained
her mind as well as her windows
with white net

in those respectable houses
plotted in military rows.
He went on asking;

took me to playgrounds urging me
to swing high for the wind
to bell my skirts out wide

for his shamed eyes.
My parents asked me why
I hated him.

And when he died he left
my son his medals and an MBE
for 'service to community'.

We found a tattered notebook
brown, HMSO, with cryptic sentences
"Arnheim. Today more shelling. Rain."

Press cuttings, photographs,
the relics of a stolen childhood—
easier now to understand.

But still I feel the clamp of his arm
when I see a girl on a swing
and an old man watching.

Uncle John

He was itinerant.
Turned up every winter month
on the back step.
Sober he'd ask—
shame-spoken—
for 'a few crumbs'.

Later, outside the warmth
of tea and cake
he'd go singing away
down the cold lanes.
Christian's Awake! he sang.
A church tenor.

Drunk, he would stand
beyond the gate
violent in prophecy.
His dust-grey dreadlocks
flung back, bottle in hand
his fierce eyes
roaring between hair and beard.

He was the family conscience
we were told.
Not to be mentioned.
Lying at last like old clothes
between the bin and step—
his hair crumbed with snow.

Tempting Fate

For Annie Sutherland

She kept a broom behind the door
to sweep away unwanted guests
and sprinkled spilt salt over
her left shoulder for the Devil,

avoided the green coat
bought before her husband died,
touched wood and counted magpies —
one for sorrow, two for joy.

White heather on the mantlepiece,
May blossom always outside
red and white flowers never
in the same vase or someone died
before the moon waned.

Two teaspoons on a saucer,
tripping upstairs meant
something borrowed, something blue —
but never marry in black
or wish yourself back.

The year the clock stopped
and she put her own foot first
through the door on New Year's Eve
she knew would bring the black-haired man
with owls' feathers in his pockets
to steal her soul.

The Godmother

She was there at my birth:
the story-teller—
bone-woman,
mouthing her hag-lore
over my cradle.

Since then I've
tried to avoid her,
deaf to her deep song,
singing my real name
outside the door.

Her voice is willow root,
a stone at the bottom of the well.

She sings me crazy days
between days, each word
a note on a stave;
each phrase a harmony.

When I wake in the night
I feel her breath
against my window.
If I dared open it
she'd witch me off
on the back of the wind.

Appleby Horse Fair

They wake me early, cantering
along the river-bank below my window;
testy stallions and barrel-bellied mares
with soft mouths and feathered shins,
bare-backed by Irish gypsies
over for the Fair.

Later I watch the pure-bred
horses harnessed in sulkies
jouncing across the grass,
arching their necks and lifting
their polished hooves like gods
from old mythologies.

In my house their ancestors gallop
under the floor. Five horses heads;
ivory shells of thin bone, blank sockets rearing
up at me out of another time.
Shaman's stallions, carrying souls to heaven.
Five white horses: one

to protect each corner of the house, one more
to bring fertility, sacrificed at the fall
of the year. Their shoes are above the door.
Their manes and tails pack the space
between my floor boards —
curl in the plastered wall.

Outside I watch them turn and trot,
hock deep in foaming water,
"broken to harness" under the whip —
flesh and sinew sold on a hand-clap.
At night I hear their mythic hooves
beating on wood; their snorting breath.

Afraid of the Dark

Best not to walk
these woods
in darkness.

The mind projects
its own horrors
on the blank screen
of the night.

A rapist crouches
fingering his garotte
or kitchen knife
promising a fate worse
than death

and monsters with yellow
eyes that burn–
the worm
who flies by night
and sucks your soul

out of your skull
and leaves the husk
to wander
as a mindless zombie.

Watch your back
as the dusk
begins to smudge the trees,
drifting across
the river bank like smoke.

The Soul Catcher

When the moon is risen
I set my snare in the bush
not caring whose soul
I net, fat or thin.

Bird or butterfly,
they shrivel above the fire
while their owner sleeps.

When the souls leave
their bone houses
I am waiting for them,

baiting my traps with hooks
and knives and the rank odours
of rotting fruit.

My charms are more powerful
than any amulet
or medicine.

When you look at the moon remember
I have souls I can sell you
for the usual fee —
should you have lost yours.

Breathing in

like the slide of water
under a bridge;
the static cling
of silk lingerie on skin,

sensually
irresistibly

this feeling
comes. I touch something–

abstract
anonymous.

Can I hold this
sense of things happening
out of sight?

The dark interior
of a magician's hat.
Numinous.

Found in A Second-hand Bookshop

'To Julia, with love from Mummy. 1931'

Lines of neat copperplate
mark Pavlova's art deco 'Life'.
A home made book-plate

promises to 'keep and treasure'
in Julia's childish hand—
pencilled ambitions underlined

'Art is hard work . . . you must not
think of self . . be practical . .
dreaming is useless . .'

On pages rubbed and frayed
the illustrations peel
from double-sided tape
as teetering ballerinas dance

through Julia's fantasies.
Saturday class. Pink satin shoes—
the rasp of sugared net.

'Art is hard work.'
The pages slip and curl.

An Emphasis of Want

For Christina Rossetti

There were no birthdays
in that narrow house
whose silence, curtained windows
and the senile mutterings of three old women
muffled the words
that crawled painfully from her pen.

Not surprising that she wrote of absence.
Two lovers and a sister dead,
Elizabeth Siddal's suicide,
Lucy Madox Brown's consumption,
Dante Gabriel thrust violently out of life
by laudanum and whisky–
and not one Pre-Raphaelite
at the funeral.

Not much like the beginning–
the dreaming virgin painted by her brother,
Hunt's radiant Christ,
Madox Brown and Swinburne at the door,
Millais and Morris and Burne Jones
bringing embroidered silks and tapestries.

Too shy to meet the Brownings
and the Poet Laureate
she stayed at home
creating goblins in the notebook
Ruskin disapproved of–
'. . . . *so full of quaintness and offence . . .*
no publisher would take them.'

Italian sensuality corseted in black,
a tongue tied by formality,
concealed her passionate poetry,
erotic fruit, burned letters,
the home for prostitutes in Highgate.

Till, broken by the stress of flesh and faith,
the worship of a sacrificial God
who wanted everything,
she lay, eaten by cancer, terrified
she had not sacrificed enough—
had kept back just one metaphor
too many, screamed
to watch hell's creatures
obscenely cavorting on her bed
and no one there but the maid
to stand between her
and the death she waited for.

Enemy Territory

This is the place I wanted to come to;
the very hotel room I imagined.

Here, yesterday, I buried my brother.
Six came to the funeral in dark jackets.

You turn down the coverlet gently
exposing the whiteness of this linen

I will soon print with my body
and carry away in my suitcase

because it holds the scent of you
to wrap me on single nights when

the absence of you gapes like the grave
I filled yesterday with a double grief.

I will not say goodbye. Not yet,
not in this city. Tomorrow

I'll put my passport in my case
for yet another destination.

How many nationalities, how many borders?
This crossing only needs no visas.

Walking Naked

When I walk naked
his eyes follow me
from the bed

He will never once say
I want you or
I love you

Words.

When the light is out
his fingers track my skin
dictating their own
erotic message

I try to answer
I do not want you
do not love you

do not want
do not love

But I do.

Predecessors

There are ghosts in these rooms;
perpetual, ageless women
whose photographs look up at me
out of forgotten drawers.

I find their earrings
down the sides of chairs;
hairs on a brush; notes
pressed between the pages
of a book autographed 'with love'.

They share the same name
these jealous figments.
On the lips of friends,
or on the phone
they have substance enough to hurt.

When I lift my arm
to take a mug from the hook
I brush their fingers; follow
their footprints out into
the garden. Their kiss

from the wet honeysuckle
on the wall, presses
as if from his mouth
who calls me, absently,
by another name.

I perform an exorcism
with hoovers, bin liners
for Oxfam, discovering

my predecessor's tampons
in a bathroom cabinet.

When I bleed I think of her
lying between us in these sheets.
We share her like a terrible dream.

Barley Silk

A loosely woven shift of colour
as the wind's sly shuttle
threads the grain's
green warp with gold
against the August light.

'To the Gods the Shades'

Inscription on a 1st century Roman tombstone in Hexham.

The wolf and wild boar wintered here
where Flavinus' impetuous latin blood
felt the unkindness of snow

and the granite hardness of the Wall
whose builders he defended against
the brutal insurgence of Pict and Celt.

Days of cracked leather, blistered hands,
the horses' breath rising like bath-house steam,
a northern mist obscuring the sun's retina;

remembering the soft, olive-perfumed
flesh of southern lovers in the rough,
hessian coupling of Celtic women —

the wire-boned, woad-stained, spoils of war,
who worshipped alien Gods and stank
of semen and ambiguous politics.

Flavinus, Standard-Bearer to the Troop —
speared by the carved barbarian
trampled under his horse — killed

by the cold driven in on the east wind
scouring the Tyne gap through this bleak
border town where everything closes at five —

his final dread — to leave his bones
to winter north in the sour peat, covered
by the same grey stone he died for.

Above Middleton

From this hill the view is larger than God,
the weather less forgiving.

Rough land, honed by a battering wind
that thrums over the houses
and howls inside the head like a chained dog.

This is the cold that cracks stone,
breaks open keens on calloused fingers
for the few descendants of the long-forgotten dead

who moled the lead seams under the Pennines,
leaving their poisoned bones
in unmarked graves.

Their cottages are fallen stone
and the roofless church
has a congregation of nettles.

They lived, not without language
or music, or the violence
of loving and birthing and hunger.

Only a death brought them down,
ill-suited in their mildewed best
to walk twelve miles to church -

buried, christened, married in job lots.
Crossing their brief marks against the register
of unrecorded lives.

Even their work is hidden

in pipes, drains, the linings of coffins,
or beaten flat in the gutters

of redundant churches, divers' boots,
the hems of old velvet curtains, fishermen's weights,
the deadly interior of a nuclear flask.

Listening to Glenn Gould on Orton Scar

From Ravenstonedale
driving north on unfenced roads,
moonlight reflects the tarmac's

frozen wake across the moor —
a snail's trail in my rear-view mirror.

·Bach unwinds from the cd
a landscape of variations
into this zero night.

The grass is white; trees black.
The walls run off like staves.

The moon fingers each stone
separately, in unexpected harmonies
and structures, endlessly practising —

compelling me to stop. Listen
to the quiet significance of the moment.

Across the counterpoint
I hear the chill cry of a predatory bird.
Single notes glitter like frost.

Winter Light

Horizontal strobes
across the russeting slope

disclose the contours of the land

the fierce geography of rock
the patterning of sheep through bracken
lipped water-marks on sand

The mountain's shadow
bruises the lake.

The season is wintering in

and the cold is like loss:
a cramping hold on bone
muscle, thought, spilling in

from the east.

The air tastes metallic
like snow dissolving on the tongue.

This is the death month
December's Druid alphabet
that signified

the rebirth of the spirit.

Ash trees clumsy with unshed seeds,
a deer's tooth grooving the bark.
I glimpse a snowdrop spiking up

through a dead leaf

before the falling sun herds
us into the longest night.

On Leaving Children

You always imagined *they*
would be the ones to leave
with tears and suitcases.
Not you, packing the car at night
taking only what you know
they won't need.

Not good at leaving are you?
Unrehearsed.
Tripped by that long cord
you thought was cut at birth
still pulsing with maternal blood.

Clumsy with failure
star of your own tragedy
you step out into childless silence
bereaved by your own exit.

Whale Music

How my flesh is split by it still! —
that giving birth to the self that isn't self,
but is so part of it that when she falls
I bruise.

Now the telephone's umbilical line
is all that connects us; travelling
sound across oceans like
whale music;

a mournful echo magnifying separation.
'I'm fine,' I tell her. 'Everything's fine.'
Practising to protect each other
we deny.

Her familiar image laughs from a shelf.
But this child-woman is a stranger — so fragile
I'm afraid. Even her voice terrifies
by omission.

I watch them in trains, cafes,
waiting rooms — mothers and daughters
locked in the terrible chemistry of relationship
and wonder

why no one warns you that the small terrorist
tumbling inside its amniotic sac
will hold your whole life
hostage.

Elizabeth's Story

You were my first-born, late-born son.
A gift
concealed beneath my skirt
when Herod's men stood at the door—
like Rachel
crouching on the stool
that kept her stolen birthright,
claiming Custom of Women.

And certainly
I smelt of woman's mysteries,
the birth-blood and the milk

And John
swaddled between my thighs
quiet
as if waiting for another birth.

A miracle.

These were the family infections—
miraculous births,
familiarity with angels,
a subversive streak.

My kinswoman and I were powerful women
who practised our own rebellions,
kept our own counsels.

We had imagined our sons differently,
taking their fathers' places.
But hers, already turning

water into wine,
disputing the prophets
with the priests,

and mine
(she grieved with me)
choosing the wilderness
beyond the Jordan,
living on locusts
and wild honey.

2

She stood with me that day
incredulous among the crowd
to hear him cry:

`Behold I come to prepare the way'

And then that trick of the light,
the clouds parting,
the shaft of sun on their heads
and the bird pausing in flight

dazzled.

Afterwards we both wondered
what we had seen.

What can I write of Herod Antipas?
camel-driver,
child-killer,
lover of his brother's wife,

throne-thief.
Inflamed by lust
he murdered my son at last
blaming the women.

Some say it was Herodias.
And some recall a promise to Salome.
Incestuous daughter and
adulterous wife.
But it was Herod's man
who stood at the door
with a sword.
My three-score breasts
dripped milk
staining my linen
when I swaddled John's
divided body
in the cloth.

But I told no-one,
being tired of miracles.

3

And after more than 30 years
of trouble
I am left alone
in this high-shuttered room
still perfumed by the gifts
of frankincense and myrrh
that Mary brought
to honour him.

(Hail Mary, full of grace,
for she has other sons.)

No angels lately come
to gild this empty space
and my womb
dry as a winter gourd.

Terremoto

Camaiore: May 2010

Today I felt the earth shudder
under my bare foot and
my head was dizzy as a ship at sea.

A cup shuffled along the shelf
and a green lemon dropped from the tree and rolled
across the cracked marble of the terrace.

For a second I was arrested
in the moment of lifting a jug of iced
water that slopped over the rim onto my toes.

The roof-tiles chattered as if
someone was running a thumb along the edge
of a deck of cards at Scopa.

And then a pause - everything still.
A breeze fluttering the leaves of the olive trees.
Everything as it was before, except

that the rock I am standing on has shifted
a centimetre further south and,
bare-foot, jug in hand, my life has moved with it.

The Reluctant Moon

Camaiore: June, 2010

The old moon is careful
       peering over the dark rim of the hill
edging out of cover
       into the open sky
the pale, cratered disc exposed
       to the prurient eye of the telescope.

I too have secrets—
damage I would not display
       for close inspection.
A life blown across my face
       by solar wind
scored, to the bedrock.

Now I am past the full
       Earth's pull is relentless
dragging us through
       all our phases
solitary - naked as the moon
hallucinating in its aura of vapour.

Queen Meave Walked Upon this Strand[1]

Queen Meave walked
her feet walked
upon
this strand
of sand
and her hair
streamed on the salt
wave of the wind
of the sea wind
that blurred
the blue
blue-green distances
between
the sky and the wild
water that waved
to the curve
of the sand
under her feet
when she walked
Queen Meave
walked
upon this strand.

And I chose you - my wild boy
and gave you the friendship of my thighs
for it was you only that could match my distances
and the multiplication of my resources.
And you matched me, ring for ring,
flock for flock, herd for herd—
Mistress of myself by mother right—
no niggardly Queen, I.

1   From a painting by Jack Yeats

How can a man know
what a woman is?
She is a language - a country,
a boat that will carry you
from yourself.
Familiar and alien . . .

I have seen you reflected
in the sheen on the still water;
tasted you in the bitter peat smoke,
my King of the nine kings.
And all the wild hours
I held you thigh-fast
bearing the print of you in my body . . .

. . . . the Lunar Queen
with her rod of lilies . . .

For mine is the ecstasy of the spirit,
the secret door that opens.
I am the beauty of the green earth
and the mystery of the waters,
Mother of the dark and the divine
and in the dust under my feet
are the hosts of heaven
from whom I draw down the Moon.

. . . She of the White Hands,
the Healer,
the Terrible,
the Fair.

One woman in the shadow of another . . .

Only for you my wild boy,
only for you, thigh-friend,
King of the nine kings,
cock of the couch.
Only for you will I take off
my bracelets and my robe
and my crown with the seven stars
and lead you by the left hand way . . .

Queen Meave walked
upon this strand
and her hair
streamed on the salt
wave of the wind
that blurred
the blue-green distances
between the sky
and the wild
water that waved
to the sand
under her feet
when Queen Meave walked
upon this strand.

Not saying goodbye at Gate 21

Wellington: September 2010

The final call
for boarding
hand-luggage scanned,
the last, forgotten,
canned drink binned.
I watch him through the glass
walk to the door and hand
over his printed pass.

He waves,
makes the clown's face
that means 'Cheer up,
this time, I won't be gone
for long'. He turns,
then turns back, lifts one hand
to the terrorist-proof glass. We place
palm to palm
remembered skin
on either side of the cold surface.

Abruptly,
already past tense,
he has wheeled off towards
the journey and, unlike Orpheus,
not looking back.
I watch the swerve
of his head, his coat flap. Then
 the screen says
'Gate closed. Boarded' and
I walk away with his absence.

Transformation

'I am becoming my mother' [Lorna Goodison]

Unwillingly, I recognise her face
travelling towards me
in the ruthless morning mirror—
unwelcome as old age;
inevitable as a Norse doom.

She watches me
evading transformation, painting
a careful reflection in the cold glass,
highlighting difference,

I am trying not to be her.
But sometimes, accidentally
her voice slips through
saying something about the weather,
Wrap up warm .. Let me know if you're late ..
Familiar, from the back of the car
Don't go too fast . . .

At the end of the journey she's waiting,
frail as a bird whose bones
would snap in your fist.
Her spirit drawn to a core –
a small kernel of stored energy
cheating winter's leaf drop.

Her younger hands reach out.
I am wearing them like gloves—
big-knuckled, fine-skinned, meshed by veins.

The Laying out of the Dead

I

The night before she died
I crept into her bed
and took the bones of her hands
between my palms and warmed them.

Now I am my mother's mother
cradling her body like a child's
watching the luminous digits
of the clock counting down her life.
No sound but the click of the morphine
pump and her lungs wrenching each breath.

I hold her delicately, conscious
of the thinness of skin, the brittleness of bone.
My cheek rests on her hair. I want her
to know I am there. But her fingers are
already slackening from my hold.

II

She used to laugh and tell me how
when I was small
I'd wriggle from her grasp
and toddle off—
'I couldn't turn my back,' she said
'Or you'd be out the door!'
The chicken house, a neighbour's garden
fields of cows. 'My heart
was in my mouth,' she said.

I can't be sure if these are memories
or told stories I've rehearsed.

III

One that is mine: fourteen, wanting to race headlong into
my self - contemptuous of my mother's warnings of the life
I longed to plunge into like a swimming pool and splash off
towards the deep end.

Visiting relatives, we shared a bed and I lay sleepless through
the night, disgusted by her nearness and the nylon nightdress
sparking static in the dark, the animal heat of her body, the
Lily of the Valley scent she dabbed on pulse points as she'd
read in magazines and called Muguet des Bois.

I lay awake and listened as the breath fluttered from her open
mouth.

IV

This is a ritual as old as life
the laying out of the dead.

I sponge the skin – slack on her bones
and baggy like an old jumper,
unravelling to expose
the heroism of her body–
the scars of childbearing
 and surgical procedure.

I push an arm into a sleeve, awkward

as a reluctant schoolchild who refuses to dress,
remembering her patience as my clumsy hands
pinched skin to bone lifting her
from chair to bed. Now
I can't hurt her.

V

What was it held me back
from talking about death?
Or love? While both of us
had breath?

Her body has gone cold, flesh
slumped towards the pull of gravity.
Redundant feet tied at the ankle, two
reproachful sentries at the bottom of the bed.

And in the drawer, a letter talks of
two dead husbands and the absent son.
'You've been the best thing in my life,' she said.

The View From Here

Arctic light cuts the ridge-backs of
the mountains black against the distance.
Climbing late on a borrowed day, we watch
a pale sun colour the near fells
buttermilk, sketching the coarse tufts
of winter grass against a blur
of wind-burned heather.

Up the shale of the last slope—
a natural slag heap, scraping
under our feet - the frozen traceries
of lingering snow glitter and crack.

The summit survey point;
scored like a sundial
with remembered distances,
angles of view
that tell you where you are,
how far it is
from where you were.

Lucidly marking out
familiar farms I left
and couldn't go back to
still in their proper places—
who I was then, am now
suddenly together here.

Three thousand and fifty feet below,
the lakes drain light from the sky
and the Solway is a slow furnace-pour
powered by the sun. Going down

fast, against the turn of the earth
the mountain's shadow rushes in front of us,
advancing faster than our feet,
the dark drifting in behind the walls
and a swollen moon rising over Carrock.